Jesus

The light in the Darkness

Intro

Who is this Jesus - We all have been told about him at some point in our lives and most of us has been told about how God sent him to the earth to heal and save the world from man's sin, but who was he. Most scholars assume his birth was between 6 and 4 BC ((BC) Before Christ Birth), and that Jesus' preaching began around 27 - 29 AD ((AD) After Christ Birth) and lasted one to three years.
He is also known as Jesus Christ, Jesus of Galilee, or Jesus of Nazareth. He is the light in the world and the only way to heaven.

In this book we will look at some aspects of Jesus' life and what it says in the bible about him.

For an event that supposedly never happened there are many relict's left over that point to Jesus and how to live a right life dedicated to following him and his teachings. The Bible is inspired by God and written by real people who had encounters and experiences with Jesus and God, the father. One can't live by bread alone but by every word of the Lord written in his word, the bible.

Free Will

God gave man Free will.

A non believer would say:
To follow God,
You have to surrender your
Free Will
and blindly follow God's Teachings.

The reality is
by following
God.
You are exercising your
Free Will.

John 12:36-37

36 Believe in the light while you have the light, so that you may become children of light." When he had finished speaking, Jesus left and hid himself from them.

37 Even after Jesus had performed so many signs in their presence, they still would not believe in him.

Faith

Is seeing
Light
With your Heart,
when all your eyes
see is darkness

Psalm 37:23-24

23 The steps of a *good* man are ordered by the Lord, And He delights in his way. **24** Though he fall, he shall not be utterly cast down; For the Lord upholds *him with* His hand.

"I am the true vine"
JOHN 15:1-5

"I am the bread of life"
JOHN 6:35-48

"I am the way, the truth and the life"
JOHN 14:6

The seven "I AM" statements of Jesus

"I am the light of the world"
JOHN 8:12; 9:5

"I am the resurrection and the life"
JOHN 11:25

"I am the good shepherd"
JOHN 10:11-14

"I am the gate"
JOHN 10:7

Psalm 34:4-8

4 God met me more than halfway, he freed me from my anxious fears.

5 Look at him; give him your warmest smile. Never hide your feelings from him.

6 When I was desperate, I called out, and God got me out of a tight spot.

7 God's angel sets up a circle of protection around us while we pray.

8 Open your mouth and taste, open your eyes and see - how good God is. Blessed are you who run to him.

If God chose you to be found in him before the foundations of the world then he already saw an ending long before you ever arrived.

God is outside of time, flesh is not, the only one surprised here is you. The only one who doesn't know the ending is you. He chose to love you long before you arrived, he saw your mistakes long before you arrived and he was pleased with his choice.

When will we understand God does not make mistakes, people do. Oh and God made allowances for those too.

Acts 16:30-31 "Sirs, what must I do to be saved?" So they said, "Believe on the Lord Jesus Christ, and you will be saved, you and your household."

John 15:16

16 You did not choose Me but I chose you, and appointed you that you would go and bear fruit, and that your fruit would remain, so that whatever you ask of the Father in My name He may give to you.

Acts 4:10

10 let it be known to all of you and to all the people of Israel, that by the name of Jesus Christ the Nazarene, whom you crucified, whom God raised from the dead—by this name this man stands here before you in good health.

You are my *Shield*,
my *Strength*, my
Portion, my *Shelter*,
my *Strong Tower* and
my *Deliverer*.
Jesus

Revelation 22:17

17 The Spirit and the bride say, "Come!" And let the one who hears say, "Come!" Let the one who is thirsty come; and let the one who wishes take the free gift of the water of life.

The world may drag you down
a hundred times

but GOD will always be there to lift you up
a thousand times

Luke 11:34-35

34 Your eye is the lamp of your body. When your eyes are healthy, your whole body also is full of light. But when they are unhealthy, your body also is full of darkness.

35 See to it, then, that the light within you is not darkness.

2 Corinthians 5:21

21 " For He made Him who knew no sin to be sin for us, that we might become the righteousness of God in Him."

Isaiah 53

6 We all, like sheep, have gone astray,
each of us has turned to our own way;
and the Lord has laid on him
the iniquity of us all.

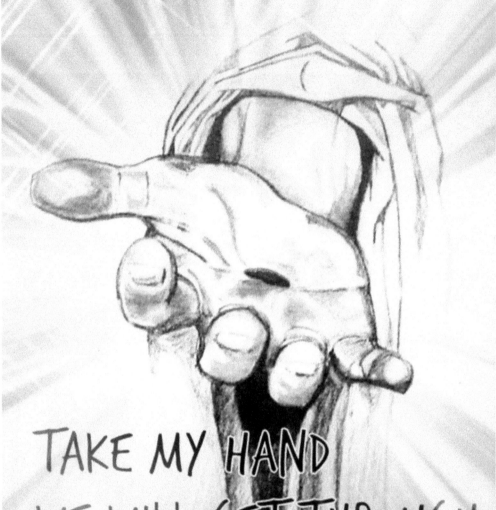

Romans 10:9-10 "That if you confess with your mouth, "Jesus is Lord," and believe in your heart that God raised him from the dead, you will be saved. For it is with your heart that you believe and are justified, and it is with your mouth that you confess and are saved."

Matthew 28:18-20

18 Then Jesus came to them and said, "All authority in heaven and on earth has been given to me. **19** Therefore go and make disciples of all nations, baptizing them in the name of the Father and of the Son and of the Holy Spirit, **20** and teaching them to obey everything I have commanded you. And surely I am with you always, to the very end of the age."

Isaiah 53:5

5 But he was pierced for our transgressions,
   he was crushed for our iniquities;
the punishment that brought us peace was on him,
   and by his wounds we are healed.

Isaiah53:1-3

1 Who has believed our message
   and to whom has the arm of the Lord been revealed?
2 He grew up before him like a tender shoot,
   and like a root out of dry ground.
He had no beauty or majesty to attract us to him,
   nothing in his appearance that we should desire him.
3 He was despised and rejected by mankind,
   a man of suffering, and familiar with pain.
Like one from whom people hide their faces
   he was despised, and we held him in low esteem.

Psalm 34:4-8

God is not a spirit of fear. He makes a way for everyone. Its like a man who is hanging off a cliff calling for help, and someone comes along with a hot air balloon and says to the man, here hop in and the man says back no I'm waiting for God to save me, another person comes along with a really big ladder and they say to him, here climb down and the man says no I'm waiting for God to save me. So the man falls and dies, when he gets to heaven. He says to God why didn't you come to save me. God says back, "but I did, I sent the man in the hot air balloon and the really big ladder. You didn't trust me that I would supply all your needs, I make all things good, All things are possible, for those who love me. I created doctors and scientists." God makes a way. He says if you take the steps towards me, I will meet you halfway. I will make a way for you. He says don't look to the left don't look to the right, don't look at those things, Just keep your eyes on me and look straight ahead and follow me.

Revelation 22:13-16

13 I am the Alpha and the Omega, the First and the Last, the Beginning and the End.

14 "Blessed are those who wash their robes, that they may have the right to the tree of life and may go through the gates into the city. **15** Outside are the dogs, those who practice magic arts, the sexually immoral, the murderers, the idolaters and everyone who loves and practices falsehood.

16 "I, Jesus, have sent my angel to give you[a] this testimony for the churches. I am the Root and the Offspring of David, and the bright Morning Star."

Links

Old Hymns
List of old Hymns in english
https://www.songandpraise.org/old-hymns/old-hymns-index.htm

Presence Christian Church
For messages and other worship
https://www.facebook.com/PresenceChristianChurch/

All the Lyrics
Songs and music
https://www.allthelyrics.com/lyrics/gospel

Bible Verses
https://www.biblegateway.com/

Know your Bible
https://bible.knowing-jesus.com/

Video This Blood
https://www.youtube.com/watch?v=u07ekuy_T6s&t=417s

Impact Church
for messages and songs
https://www.facebook.com/impactchurch.au/

Can you imagine what it would have been like... Put yourself in his shoes for just a minute.

You have just been whipped with every razor sharp lash, every stroke of unbearable pain reaching deep down as each lashes of tightly woven chips of bone rip your skin open, causing blood to flow. You're tossed about as if you were just a toy, to be beaten to a pulp and if that wasn't enough they forced a needle sharp spiked crown of thorns upon your head. Piercing your skin and splintering deep into your skull, blood dripping from the punctured holes. You're matted hair hangs limply down, soaked and dripping with your blood, you gaze out through stunned and shocked eyes. Longing for a drink that would never come, you're pushed out the gate.
Only to be faced with a heavy sturdy build wooden cross towering over you waiting for you to carry it to your doom.

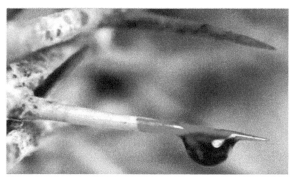

We can only imagine what Jesus went through, what suffering he put up with for you and me. To be that bridging gap between God and man and he did it all for us.
Is your un-belief worth testing, are you willing to stand before the throne of God at the end of your days and still say you do not believe.

We can't handle a single paper cut or a splinter in our hands without flinching in pain. Yet this man, they called Jesus, took all of that pain and more for you and me.

He carried that cross upon his shoulder up hill in a extremely weakened state with the crown of thorns digging deeper into his skull as the cross lent against his shoulder and head and yet we can't handle a single headache.

Imagine having large rough nails hammered over and over through your hands and feet until they were fastened tightly to the cross. Every inch of his body shook with pain after every blow.

We all have the right to choose, to choose to believe or not. Its like choosing which airline you are going to fly with, which destination you are going to end up at when you leave this life of yours.

Revelation 3:20
20 "Behold, I stand at the door and knock. If anyone hears my voice and opens the door, I will come in to him and eat with him, and he with me."

Amazing Grace

Amazing grace! How sweet the sound
That saved a wretch like me!
I once was lost, but now am found;
Was blind, but now I see.

Through many dangers, toils and snares,
I have already come;
'Tis grace hath brought me safe thus far,
And grace will lead me home.

The Lord has promised good to me,
His Word my hope secures;
He will my Shield and Portion be,
As long as life endures.

Yea, when this flesh and heart shall fail,
And mortal life shall cease,
I shall possess,
within the veil,
A life of joy and peace.

The earth shall soon dissolve like snow,
The sun forbear to shine;
But God, who called me here below,
Will be forever mine.

When we've been there ten thousand years,
Bright shining as the sun,
We've no less days to sing God's praise
Than when we'd first begun.

John Newton, 1725-1807

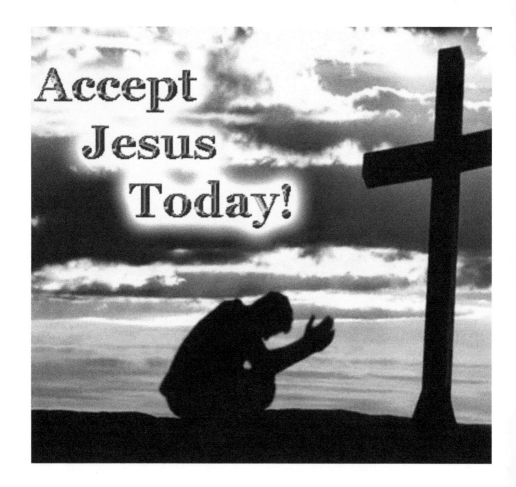

In this time of great sorrow and despair we all need a comforting heart where we can feel safe and Jesus can give that to us even with our last breath, on your death bed.

Sinner Prayer
Dear Lord Jesus, I know that I am a **sinner**, and I ask for Your forgiveness. I believe You died for my sins and rose from the dead. I turn from my sins and invite You to come into my heart and life. I want to trust and follow You as my Lord and Savior.

If you have prayed this pray, know you will be safe in the Lord Jesus's arms and you will get to see your family again in heavenly places.

John 5:24 "Truly, truly, I say to you, whoever hears my word and believes him who sent me has eternal life. He does not come into judgment, but has passed from death to life."

Do it today! Don't wait till tomorrow
You could be dead.

If you have just given your heart to the Lord, let someone know,
Here are some places to tell
https://www.facebook.com/impactchurch.au/
https://www.facebook.com/EricMcDanielMinistries/
or your local church

These contacts are not associated with this book in any way shape or form

Contents

Authors other books

Santa's Happy Holidays, Aussie Style

Softcover: ISBN: 9780368162787
Hardcover, ImageWrap: ISBN: 9780368162794
https://au.blurb.com/b/9253684-santa-s-happy-holidays-aussie-style

A Humble Poetry Book

ebook: https://au.blurb.com/ebooks/552998-a-humble-poetry-book
Softcover: ISBN: 9781364822514
Hardcover, Dust Jacket: ISBN: 9781364822507
Hardcover, ImageWrap: ISBN: 9781364822521
https://au.blurb.com/b/6593017-a-humble-poetry-book

165 Ways to Make Your Heart Fly

Softcover ISBN: 9781714175802
Hardcover, Dust Jacket ISBN: 9781714175819
Hardcover, ImageWrap ISBN: 9781714175826
https://www.blurb.com/b/9685728-165-ways-to-make-your-heart-fly

Love Hurts

Softcover ISBN: 9780464591269
Hardcover, Dust Jacket ISBN: 9780464591276
Hardcover, ImageWrap ISBN: 9780464591283
https://www.blurb.com/b/9775274-love-hurts

Life Changes

Softcover: ISBN: 9780368871672
PDF: https://au.blurb.com/b/9498625-life-changes

Genealogy Made Easy

https://au.blurb.com/ebooks/605105-genealogy-made-easy
Softcover: ISBN: 9781366710710
Hardcover, Dust Jacket: ISBN: 9781366710703
Hardcover, ImageWrap: ISBN: 9781366710727
PDF: https://au.blurb.com/b/7566791-genealogy-made-easy

Psychology of Thinking 1

A Collective of Poems

ebook: https://au.blurb.com/ebooks/551302-psychology-of-thinking-1
Softcover: ISBN: 9781364874094
Hardcover, Dust Jacket: ISBN: 9781364874070
Hardcover, ImageWrap: ISBN: 9781364874087
PDF: https://au.blurb.com/b/6564432-psychology-of-thinking-1

Looking Up

PDF: https://au.blurb.com/b/9920363-looking-up
Softcover: *ISBN: 9781714329267*
Hardcover Dust Jacket: *ISBN: 9781714329243*
Hardcover ImageWrap: *ISBN: 9781714329250*
ebook: https://au.blurb.com/ebooks/715407-looking-up

Tasmania's Cradle

https://au.blurb.com/ebooks/541334-tasmania-s-cradle
Softcover: ISBN: 9781320488358
Hardcover, ImageWrap: ISBN: 9781320488365
PDF: https://au.blurb.com/b/6394771-tasmania-s-cradle

South Australia - In Picture Form Vol 1

ebook: https://au.blurb.com/ebooks/618082-south-australia
Softcover: ISBN: 9781366254474
Hardcover, ImageWrap: ISBN: 9781366254481
PDF: https://au.blurb.com/b/7800155-south-australia

Santa Brings on Christmas

ebook: https://au.blurb.com/ebooks/709285-santa-brings-on-christmas
Softcover ISBN: 9780464525301
Hardcover, ImageWrap ISBN: 9780464525295
PDF: https://www.blurb.com/b/9749157-santa-brings-on-christmas

Provoking the Senses

Softcover ISBN: 9780464621935
Hardcover, Dust Jacket ISBN: 9780464621959
Hardcover, ImageWrap ISBN: 9780464621942
https://www.blurb.com/b/9789708-provoking-the-senses

Walk the Narrow Path to Righteousness

ebook: https://au.blurb.com/ebooks/600796-walk-the-narrow-path-to-righteousness
Softcover: ISBN: 9781366874528
Hardcover, Dust Jacket: ISBN: 9781366874535
Hardcover, ImageWrap: ISBN: 9781366874511
PDF: https://au.blurb.com/b/7462178-walk-the-narrow-path-to-righteousness

Shark Attack

ebook: https://au.blurb.com/ebooks/691195-shark-attack
Softcover: ISBN: 9780368407543
Hardcover, ImageWrap: ISBN: 9780368407536
PDF: https://au.blurb.com/b/9344014-shark-attack

Fun Fact of Christmas

Softcover: ISBN: 9780464650898
Hardcover, Dust Jacket: ISBN: 9780464650904
Hardcover, ImageWrap: ISBN: 9780464650911

The Virtual Tour, Book 1

ebook: https://au.blurb.com/ebooks/720705-the-virtual-tour-book-1
Softcover: ISBN: 9781714642014
Hardcover, Dust Jacket: ISBN: 9781714642021
Hardcover, ImageWrap: ISBN: 9781714642038
PDF: https://au.blurb.com/b/10028326-the-virtual-tour-book-1

Directional
History
Travel
Spiritual
Poetry
Genealogy
Photography

Enjoyable   Read   Life
         Author   Pen
                    ISBN
                         Print
                         Books
         Story
              Reading   Ink

https://au.blurb.com/user/Ecaabooks   eBooks

                    Writing

CPSIA information can be obtained
at www.ICGtesting.com
Printed in the USA
LVHW071611220520
656048LV00003BA/343

9 781714 775866